The Moon Maiden
& Other Asian Folktales

by Hua Long

China Books & Periodicals, Inc.
San Francisco   1993

We would like to thank Magareta and Chris Noyes for all their support on this project, Greg Jones for making it all happen, Casandra Jones for editorial assistance, and the instructors at Academy of Art College of San Francisco for helping to develop our skills as artists.

*Hua Long i*s a collective of illustrators and artists based in the San Francisco Bay Area. The name *Hua Long* comes from the Chinese idiom *"Hua Long Dian Jing,"* which translates literally as "adding the eyes on a painted dragon," and means adding the finishing touches on a work. *Hua Long* is Nancy Chen, Daniele Fraboulet, Kosal Kong, Yumiko Konishi, Victor Lee, Wendy K. Lee, Quan Van Nguyen, Azusa Omura, Peggy Smith, Heather Snitzer, Hanako Wakiyama, and Ray Wong.

Art Editor   Wendy K. Lee
Book Designer   Linda Revel
Cover illustration by Nancy Chen
Title page illustration by Heather Snitzer
Back cover illustration by Daniele Fraboulet

1 3 5 7 9 10 8 6 4 2

First Edition 1993

Library of Congress Catalog Card Number 93-072096

ISBN 0-8351-2493-2 (paperback)
ISBN 0-8351-2494-0 (cloth)

Printed in Hong Kong by Regent Publishing Services, Ltd.

TABLE OF CONTENTS

Peacock with the Fiery Tail

THE PEACOCK FAIRY had the head and arms of a beautiful woman, but had a peacock's tail and body. All of the peacocks in the world wanted to be her apprentice and learn some of her magic tricks. One day she brought them all together.

"I know you all want to be my apprentice, but I can only choose one of you, and you all look alike," she said. "I want you to all come back to me at midnight, and don't all look the same!"

They all left making plans to make themselves more beautiful and stand out from the crowd. But one good-hearted little peacock thought to himself, "I am such an ordinary peacock, there is no hope for me. I'll just go on my way and not worry about it."

He started walking and soon he met an old man on the road who was hot and sweating. Little Peacock gave him some of his tail feathers to make a fan and cool him off. The old man thanked him, but Little Peacock just said, "Don't mention it."

Then he met a pretty young girl, crying by the roadside. When he asked what the matter was, she said, "My stepmother makes me work all the time, and gives me old clothes to wear. I have been asked to a dance by a handsome boy, and I have nothing good to wear. Without a word, Little Peacock pulled some feathers from his tail, and gave them to her, to put in her hair and cover her gown. She thanked the peacock again and again, but he just went on his way.

And so it went the rest of the day, with Little Peacock giving away all his plumes to help people in need. Near dark, he overheard voices from a hut along the road. A little boy said, "Mommy, I know I must stay in bed to get better, but I know if I see fireworks at the festival I will be well. Can't I see the fireworks now?"

"But my child, they don't set off the fireworks until the festival starts, and it is too early for the festival," answered his mother.

When Little Peacock heard these words, his eyes filled with tears. "If only I could show him my display of feathers, he might believe they were fireworks and become well." But sadly, he realized that he had given away all his plumes.

At midnight, all the peacocks assembled before the Peacock Fairy. Some had fireflies set in their tails to look like stars, and many had put flowers in their plumes. Surely it would be difficult to choose an apprentice!

"My friends," said the Peacock Fairy, "You all look so beautiful! But I see one who looks very different from the rest. Little Peacock, come here. Where are all your feathers?" Little Peacock told his story, how he had given away all his feathers to help people. The Peacock Fairy thought for a while, then smiled and said, "Little one, you are the apprentice I want." With a wave of her hand, one plume from every peacock rose in the air and formed a large beautiful fan. Then the fan came down upon Little Peacock's tail!

"Now, I will teach you another trick," said the Peacock Fairy. She whispered magic words in his ear, and when he repeated them three times, his tail burst into a kaleidoscope of fire!

Little Peacock soared into the air, flying over all the villages with his fiery tail. When the sick little boy saw the fire in the sky, he said, "Mama, I see the fireworks! I feel better already!" The little peacock flew through the night, bringing joy and happiness throughout the land.

And so when you see fireworks exploding during festivals, look closely for the Peacock with the Fiery Tail.

illustration by Hanako Wakiyama

The Serving Maid's Parrot

ONCE UPON A TIME IN the Chinese province of Sichuan, a rich man had a beautiful and intelligent servant named Li Li. Since she was his favorite worker, he let her feed and take care of his most prized possession, a very colorful and unusual parrot.

Li Li took good care of the bird, giving it food and talking to it lovingly. One day the bird surprised her by speaking to her! "Awk!" it said. "For taking such good care of me, I will find you an excellent husband!"

"Silly bird," she said. "How can a parrot find me a husband?" The two became good friends, and spent long hours talking to each other about everything under the sun.

The parrot was so tame that Li Li never locked its cage. But one day the bird got out. Li Li tried desperately to catch the bird, but it flew around the room several times, then out a window and was gone.

Heartbroken and frightened, Li Li went to see her master to tell him the bird was gone. "It was my fault the bird flew away — you may put me to death if you wish!" The master was angry at losing his wonderful parrot, but forgave the serving maid for her honesty, and let her stay in his household. Some of the other servants became jealous of her being the master's favorite.

Some days later, Li Li was sent on an errand to the Liang family household. At his house, a young unmarried son named Liang Hsu was quietly reading in his room on the second floor, when suddenly a bright flash of feathers flew around him. "Awk!" said the parrot. "I have found a beautiful and talented wife for you. Just look out the window!"

The young man looked out the window just as Li Li was approaching the house. When he saw her face, he was struck by her beauty, and rushed down the stairs to see her. Because she was only a servant, Li Li could not talk to him, but they looked lovingly at each other.

Upon returning to her room, Li Li found the parrot sitting on its cage. "Now that I have found your husband-to-be, let me be your messenger, and carry letters between you two, telling of your love for each other."

"But if what you say is true, Liang Hsu is rich, talented, and handsome. Why would he want a poor maid like me?" asked Li Li. The bird did not answer but quickly flew away.

The parrot flew to the young man, and told him of her fears. Liang Hsu then wrote a beautiful love poem for Li Li that stated his intention to marry her. "Here! Take this to her," he said, putting the note in the bird's beak.

Arriving at Li Li's room, the parrot gave the note to her. She did not know how to read the beautiful Chinese characters, for servants were not taught to read and write. She only could show her love by sending one of her earrings to him.

illustration by Ray Wong

The parrot took the earring and flew out the window.

But on the way to Liang Hsu's house, a cruel boy threw a rock at the flying parrot. The rock hit the bird, and sent it falling to the ground, dead.

Meanwhile, some of the other servants in the household, jealous of Li Li's position in the house, spread rumors to the master that she was secretly seeing a man, for they heard her talking in the night with someone. The master searched her room, and found the letter from Liang Hsu. Li Li tried to tell the truth, but no one would believe her story about the talking parrot. She was beaten badly, then put into a coffin and buried in a nearby woods.

Word of her death spread to Liang Hsu, who cried bitterly over his lost love. That night, a woman came into his dreams. She was clothed in bright feathers, and said: "I am the parrot, and my beloved sister is the one you love. She was once a parrot also, but came back to life as a human. Unfortunately, I was killed before I could complete my task in uniting you, but she still lives, and if you hurry to the place I show you, perhaps you can save her."

In the dream, the parrot-woman showed him the place in the woods where Li Li was buried. He awoke quickly, and hurried to the burial site. Digging up the coffin, and breaking it open, he found a faint breath of life in Li Li. Taking her in his arms, he carried her home to his mother. She helped nurse Li Li back to health. Li Li married Liang Hsu, and whenever they met someone who had captured a parrot, they bought the bird and set it free, in thanks to the wonderful parrot who brought them together.

The Moon Maiden

ONE DAY THE EMPEROR of China was riding in his sedan chair when he saw a man with a huge red bow and long arrows. The Emperor had never seen a bow like it, and asked the man if he could look at it.

The man said, "I am Hou Yi, and with this bow I can shoot arrows from one side of the world to the other!"

He demonstrated his skill by shooting an arrow into a pine tree far up on a mountain top. The Emperor was so impressed, he gave him the position of Imperial Archer.

Hou Yi used his skills many times to help the people of China. When enemies attacked, he was there to drive them away. When wild animals did harm to villages, he was there to kill them. When rain did not fall, he would shoot arrows into the sky to remind the sky dragons that water was needed.

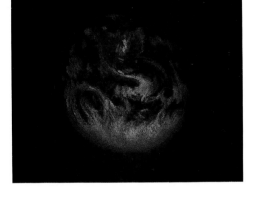

One year there was a terrible flood. Rivers spilled into fields and villages, and many people drowned. The Emperor sent Hou Yi to stop the Water Spirit who was causing the flood. Hou Yi found him and drove him away with his magic arrows, and the rivers quickly returned to normal and the villages were saved.

The Water Spirit had a beautiful sister, named Chang E. When Hou Yi saw her, he was so struck by her beauty, he instantly fell in love. He could not shoot his arrow at her, but shot instead into her thick hair she wore coiled high on her head. The maiden was so grateful to Hou Yi for sparing her life, she agreed to become his wife.

Not long after this, ten suns appeared in the sky. The heat of the sun dried leaves on their branches, burned grass blades to a crisp, and dried up the water in wells and streams. Hou Yi was called in to shoot down the extra suns before everything died beneath the scorching heat of the suns.

Hou Yi shot down the first sun. He shot a second arrow and knocked down the second sun. Three, four, five, six, seven, eight, nine suns disappeared as Hou Yi's arrows found their targets.

Hou Yi was about to shoot the tenth sun out of the sky when the Sun God said, "Wait, Hou Yi. You must leave one sun in the sky to light and warm the earth. Without a sun, no one could live on earth." So, Hou Yi left one sun shining in the sky.

One day Hou Yi went out hunting for a magic potion that would make you live forever, so that Chang E and he could be together always. He found this elixir in Kun Lun, a far western mountain, in the home of the Queen Mother of the West. She agreed to give Hou Yi the elixir, but the Queen Mother warned him, "This elixir is very rare, and I am giving you enough for two people. If one person should swallow all of it, that person would fly off to heaven. You must wait until the time is right, one year from now, before drinking it."

Hou Yi returned home, and hid the

illustration by Nancy Chen

potion in their house, waiting for the special day to share it with Chang E. She found the elixir accidentally one night while Hou Yi was away, and secretly drank all of it.

As soon as she finished drinking the potion, she felt very light. She began to float in the air, up and up into the night sky. She soared through the night, until she arrived on the cold and lonely moon. And there the Moon Maiden has stayed to this day, alone except for the white Jade Rabbit who lives there, as punishment for stealing the elixir of long life.

Hou Yi was very angry at his wife for drinking all of the elixir. The Queen Mother of the West took pity on him and gave Hou Yi more of the elixir of long life. He flew to the sun, and took with him the Queen Mother's other gift to him, a golden bird with a red comb. This golden bird, which is the ancestor of the rooster, signals the time that the sun is to rise every morning.

Hou Yi forgave his wife and built her a beautiful palace in the moon. He also arranged to visit her on the moon once a month. It is when he goes to see her on the night of the fifteenth of every month that the moon is largest and fullest. When he leaves her, the moon grows paler and paler, and it does not grow bright again until it is time for his visit once again.

Sister Lace

ONCE UPON A TIME, ON A faraway mountain in China, there was a clever girl with a special talent. She could make lace into animals that were so lifelike that people mistook them for the real thing. They called her "Sister Lace", and her fame spread throughout the land. Many others tried to copy her, but no matter how much they tried, no one could make lace as beautiful as Sister Lace. She was very generous with her skill, and swore she would teach her friends to make lace as well as she could.

When the Emperor of China heard about her, he sent his servants to fetch her, but she refused to go. "I must stay here and teach the other girls to make lace," she said.

When the Emperor heard this, he was very angry, and ordered her dragged to the Palace. When she still refused to bow down before him, he had her thrown into prison.

The next day the Emperor came to her and said, "You are very silly. If you marry me, you will have all the comfort of the Palace and want for nothing!"

Sister Lace replied, "I want to live in my village and teach my friends to make lace."

The Emperor thought a while, then said, "If you are so good at making lace, make me a live rooster from your lace in seven days. If you do, you can return home, otherwise you must live with me forever." And so she worked hard, and on the seventh day it was done. She bit her finger and let a drop of blood fall on the rooster's comb, and cried a tear into the rooster's mouth. The bird flapped its wings and crowed!

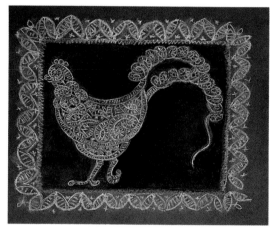

When the Emperor came in, he saw the rooster and refused to believe it had been made from lace. The rooster flew up to the Emperor's head and scratched and clawed him, then flew out the window.

"I will give you another chance," said the Emperor. "Make me a wild partridge from lace, and I will send you home."

And seven days later, Sister Lace had finished a wild partridge. She again pricked her finger and let drops of blood fall on the feathers of the bird. She cried a tear which fell into the bird's mouth, and it leaped to life.

The Emperor, upon seeing the bird, said to Sister Lace, "No, no! You misunderstood me! I said to make me a dragon!" With that, the partridge flew at the Emperor and pecked at the Emperor's head as hard as it could, then flew away.

"You have one week to make me a dragon!" The Emperor said.

And seven days later, Sister Lace had completed a small dragon. She pricked her finger, and her blood dyed the dragon red. A tear from her eye fell into its mouth, and the dragon roared alive.

When the Emperor came to see what she had made, he cried in alarm, "That's not a dragon, it's a snake!" The dragon became angry at hearing this, and spit out a huge ball of fire, which burned the Emperor and all of his men to death. Sister Lace then climbed on the dragon's back, and they flew home through the sky, leaving a trail of many colors behind them.

Even today, when you see a rainbow in the sky, you know it is the work of Sister Lace.

illustration by Peggy Smith

Golden Chisel and the Stone Ram

LONG, LONG AGO, THE water of the Zuli River tasted salty and bitter. If the villagers wanted clear water to drink, they had to travel over thirty miles to get some. An ancient prophecy foretold of a magic ram that could produce pure spring water. The villagers knew of this prophecy but did not understand it until Golden Chisel discovered its secret.

Golden Chisel was a young stone mason. He was the most skilled mason for miles and miles around. When he carved plants in stone, you could feel each leaf and branch. When he chiseled birds and beasts, they seemed to come to life.

Late in the evening one day Golden Chisel passed by a dry pond south of the village. Suddenly, he saw a spark of light in the center of the pond. Puzzled, he stood and waited for the light to flash again. A hour passed. The light did not appear again, so he went home.

Golden Chisel returned to the pond early the next day and began digging in the center of the pond where he thought he had seen the spark of light. After he removed a layer of red clay and a layer of black sand, he saw a glow coming from beneath the rocks and sand. He dug out a dazzling bright stone. Delighted, he carried it home. He studied the stone for a few days, and finally decided to carve a stone ram out of it.

Carefully, Golden Chisel carved the curved horns, the curling hair, the soft eyes and the delicate hooves from the stone. He worked nonstop for nine days and nine nights and had almost completed the ram. As soon as he added the finishing touch by carving its last hoof, the ram began wiggling its ears and blinking its eyes! The stone ram had come to life!

The little ram opened its mouth and said to Golden Chisel, "Golden Chisel, thank you for carving me! I'd like to repay you. If you need gold, I can get you gold. If you need silver, I can get you silver. I can get you whatever you need."

Golden Chisel shook his head and said, "I don't want gold or silver. I don't need anything for myself. If you can get pure spring water so that the villagers can stop drinking bitter water and enjoy the true taste of their tea and food, I shall be grateful."

The stone ram thought for a while. Blinking its eyes, it said, "You've given me a difficult assignment, but I'll try my best. You must remember not to tell our secret to anyone, for if anyone sees me and tells everyone about me, my magic will end."

Golden Chisel agreed. The little ram raced away, and in the twinkling of an eye it had run over thirty miles. It ran to the Yellow River, swallowed a bellyful of water, headed straight back to the village, and spit out the water into the dried pond. It ran back and forth three times that night until the pond was filled with clear water.

The next day the villagers were astounded. The once dry pond was full of clear sparkling water! Everyone smiled brightly as they carried water in buckets to their homes to drink and cook with. At the end of the day the pond was almost empty, but the next morning it was full again. Only Golden Chisel knew that it was the little stone ram who filled the pond three times each night with water from the Yellow River.

illustration by Victor Lee

One hundred days passed. One night the little stone ram went to fetch water as usual. The next morning when the cock crowed, the ram had not returned. Golden Chisel was very worried. He didn't know what had happened to the stone ram and went to search for it along the mountain road leading to the Yellow River. He wandered for hours before finding the ram in a gully. It was lying among the weeds, groaning, "Golden Chisel. The wicked god of the Yellow River cut off one of my hooves. I can't run anymore."

Golden Chisel picked up the little stone ram sadly and carried it home. The water in the pond gradually dried up and the villagers were without clear water once again. Golden Chisel vowed he would punish the god of the Yellow River for his wicked deed.

It took Golden Chisel several days to carve a new gold hoof for the little ram. Once he had attached the new hoof to the stone ram, he took out the Sun-and-Moon Talisman that had been handed down in his family for generations, mounted the little stone ram and rode it to the Yellow River.

The wicked god of the river was squatting on the bank with his head lowered. In one great stride, Golden Chisel leapt in front of the god and shouted, "You cut off my stone ram's hoof when all it did was take a little of your water! If you don't admit your guilt, I will burn you to ashes."

Golden Chisel's sudden appearance startled the god of the river. He pulled out the crystal sword that hung on his belt

and waved it at the young stone mason. He sneered, "How dare you talk to me like that! Who do you think you are? I will not allow you to steal my water!"

Golden Chisel shouted back, "Your water? The water of the Yellow River belongs to everyone. You have no right to keep it all for yourself!"

Unable to deny this, the god yelled at Golden Chisel, "Go away! Leave this instant or I'll blow on you and turn you into a block of ice!"

Before Golden Chisel had a chance to reply, the god opened his mouth and blew out a freezing blast of air which turned everything in its path to ice. Golden Chisel calmly took out the Sun-and-Moon Talisman and tapped it a few times. It let out a warm golden glow, and suddenly, a purple beam of light shot out from the center of the talisman and slowly spread outward, like a fan unfolding. Wherever the beam of light touched the earth the ice melted.

The god of the river, seeing his first trick defeated, summoned up thousands of vicious water sprites and turtle demons from the river. They all charged at Golden Chisel, baring their fangs and waving their claws. Golden Chisel swung the Sun-and-Moon Talisman around in the air. It gave off a streak of fire which blazed into the sky. Seeing this, the demons and ghosts dove back into the water in terror, not daring to poke their heads out. The flaming stream wound itself around the god of the river. His long beard was scorched, giving off a cloud of black smoke. The god of the river screamed in pain and dropped his crystal sword into the river.

Holding the talisman high, Golden Chisel cried, "This Sun-and-Moon Talisman is the Stone of Heavenly Fire. It can burn mountains into ash and boil the sea dry. If you don't let us use the water of the Yellow River, I shall burn you to death."

The river god lowered his head in defeat and moaned, "Mason, forgive me, please! Don't burn me! I will give you whatever you need."

Golden Chisel replied, "I only want water from the Yellow River."

The god took a pearl from his mouth and said, "This is a 'water-producing pearl'. When the stone ram holds it in his mouth, pure water will flow from it forever."

Golden Chisel took the pearl and put it in the stone ram's mouth. As soon as the stone ram opened its mouth, pure water came pouring forth like a fountain.

Dawn was breaking and a cock crowed in the distance. The stone ram said, "Brother Golden Chisel! Hurry up. If the sun comes up and someone sees us, everything will be ruined!"

Once more Golden Chisel mounted the stone ram. It ran as fast as it could, but could not run as quickly as before because of its wounded hoof. By the time they got near the village, the sun was rising above the horizon.

A young cowherd had risen early and was driving his cattle out to pasture when he saw a bright light shooting towards him from a distance. As the light moved closer the cowherd cried out without thinking, "Come and look, everyone! It's Golden Chisel riding a stone ram!"

As soon as the stone ram heard this, it stopped in its tracks. The sun rose higher in the sky and in its bright rays the stone ram was immediately transformed into a heap of rocks, from which flowed fresh clear water. To this day, the people along the river enjoy fresh water, thanks to Golden Chisel and his magic ram.

King of the Forest

LION LIVED IN THE FOREST and declared himself king of the animals. All of the animals feared Lion and dared not make him angry.

One day Elephant stomped through the forest. Lion was upset and roared at him so loudly that the whole forest shook. The smaller animals were frightened.

Swinging his trunk back and forth, Elephant went on his way. Lion pounced in front of Elephant and demanded, "Stop! How dare you make so much noise in my forest!"

Not in the least bothered by Lion's words, Elephant answered, "What? Your forest? The forest belongs to men and I carry logs for them."

Lion said coldly, "You want to work here, eh? Well, what can you do?"

"What can I do?" answered Elephant. "Do you want to compete with me?"

Lion ordered Monkey to help him picking fruit. As Monkey swung his arms up and down, fruit rained down and fell in large piles under the tree.

Then Elephant strolled up to the fruit tree. He lifted his big, heavy trunk and hit it over and over again against the tree, bringing down a shower of fruit.

Elephant won the competition and Lion's plan failed. He turned to Elephant and said, "The competition has only just begun. Follow Deer to a marshy ground not far from here and try to cross it."

Standing on the edge of the marsh, the small animals watched anxiously. Deer shivered as he put one leg in the muddy water, while Elephant crossed the marsh without hesitation. His feet were so big that he was in no danger to sinking at all.

While the animals were watching Elephant, Deer stepped in a deep hole and sank! All the small animals cried out for Elephant to save Deer.

Elephant turned around, curled his trunk around Deer's body and pulled him out of the swamp. Elephant then continued to cross the rest of the marsh with Deer in the coil of his trunk until he reached dry ground.

Lion, angry that Elephant had won once again, roared ferociously. "I'll show you a thing or two and then we'll see who is powerful enough to rule the forest!"

Lion went raging through the forest roaring at everything he passed. The wind howled in fear and the sun hid behind a cloud. The trees and the grass trembled.

Lion then said to Elephant, "Did you see that? The whole forest fears me."

"I did," replied Elephant. "But now, watch me."

Elephant curled his trunk around a huge tree and pulled it out of the ground with one tug. Then he did the same with all the other trees around him. Soon, Elephant had cut a path through the forest.

Lion could not control his temper any more. He chased the small animals, threatening to kill them all. They scattered and ran in all directions.

Seeing this, Elephant became angry. He raised his trunk, grabbed Lion tightly at the waist, lifted him up in the air, and threw him as far as he could high into the sky. Lion was never to be seen again.

The small animals, amazed by Elephant's strength, gathered around him and elected him as their king. Big Elephant declined saying, "I do not wish to be a king. I must go back to my work moving logs for men."

Picking up a big tree with his trunk, Elephant strolled off into the distance.

illustration by Kosal Kong

The Black Bear and the Fox

ONCE UPON A TIME GOAT was grazing at the foot of a mountain. Suddenly, he heard a noise. Looking up, Goat saw it was Black Bear getting ready to eat him.

Goat was very scared, but thought to himself, "Since I can't escape, what's the point of being afraid?" So, Goat pretended not to be frightened and continued to munch on the grass.

Black Bear stood in front of Goat, expecting him to run away. Since Black Bear had never seen Goat before, he wondered why Goat ignored him. Black Bear thought, "This might be a dangerous beast. I'd better ask him to identify himself."

So Black Bear mustered up some courage and, moving closer to Goat, said, "What is your name?"

Goat replied angrily, "What? You don't know my name is Mountain Goat?"

Pointing at Goat's horns, Black Bear asked, "What are those things growing out of your head?"

"Those are my double-edged swords!"

Black Bear asked, "What is that thing hanging from your behind?"

Goat wagged its tail and replied, "That's my ax!"

"What is that thing growing under your chin?" asked Black Bear.

Goat replied impatiently, "That's a napkin for wiping my mouth after eating bear fat!"

Hearing this, Black Bear was frightened and ran towards the mountain in terror.

On the way to the mountain, Black Bear passed Fox. Stopping Black Bear, Fox asked, "Brother Bear, what has given you such a fright?"

Black Bear panted, "I just ran into a horrible beast named Mountain Goat. He nearly swallowed me alive!"

Puzzled, Fox asked, "What is it like, this creature named Mountain Goat?"

Glancing behind him and seeing that Goat was no longer in sight, Black Bear relaxed and replied, "There are two double-edged swords on his head, an ax on his behind, and hanging under his chin is a cloth which he uses for wiping his mouth after eating bear fat!"

Fox burst out laughing: "Brother Bear! He's only a mountain goat! He seems terrible the way you describe him, but he is really quite harmless. Goat meat is quite delicious. Why don't we go back there together and eat him?"

Fox promised Black Bear that he was telling the truth, and Black Bear agreed to go with Fox and followed him back to eat Goat.

Having scared off Black Bear, Goat relaxed and continued eating the grass. But as he raised his head to look around, he saw Fox heading towards him with Black Bear behind him.

Goat was again terrified and thought, "That Fox is wicked. How can I keep from being eaten this time?"

Fox and Black Bear came closer and closer. Suddenly, an idea popped into Goat's head and he called out in welcome, "Brother Fox, you are truly a friend who keeps his word! I asked you to find me a bear and here you are two days ahead of schedule. Let's celebrate as we dine on bear meat and bear paws tonight!"

When he heard this, Black Bear was both angry and scared. He hit Fox on the head and fled into the mountains.

Outsmarting Black Bear once again, Goat returned home in peace.

illustration by Azusa Omura

The Dazzling Pearl

ALONG TIME AGO THERE lived a snow-white dragon known as Jade Dragon. He lived in a cave on the east bank of the Milky Way called the Celestial River. In the forest on the opposite side of the river lived Golden Phoenix.

Every morning they greeted each other before going their separate ways. One would fly in the sky while the other swam in the Celestial River. They met on an island one day, and there Golden Phoenix found a shining stone.

"Look, how beautiful this stone is," she said to Jade Dragon.

"Let's carve it into a pearl," Jade Dragon said.

Jade Dragon used his claw and Golden Phoenix her beak to grind the pebble. They ground it every day and after many years of hard work, the ball became a dazzling pearl. By now they had grown attached to each other and both loved the pearl dearly. They decided to live on the island forever, guarding the pearl.

It was a magic pearl. Wherever it shone things became better and brighter.

One day the Queen Mother of the West saw its brilliant rays of light in the sky and was so overwhelmed by its beauty that she wanted it for herself. So she sent one of her most trustworthy guards to steal the dazzling object when Golden Phoenix and Jade Dragon were asleep. After the guard stole the pearl, the Queen Mother hid it in a secret room protected by nine gates and nine locks. There she enjoyed the pearl all by herself.

When Jade Dragon and Golden Phoenix awoke and discovered that the pearl was gone, they were upset and searched everywhere but could not find the pearl. They never gave up hope that someday they would recover their treasured pearl.

Then came the birthday of the Queen Mother of the West. The immortals from all over the universe came to the palace to celebrate. She prepared a grand feast, serving her guests nectar and celestial peaches, the fruit of immortality. She drank too much wine and blurted out, "My immortal friends, I want to show you a truly precious pearl which cannot be found either in Heaven or on Earth." She then took out nine keys from her pocket and unlocked the nine gates one after another, until she reached the secret room. She put the pearl on a golden tray and carried it carefully to the table in the center of the banquet hall. The whole hall was instantly lit by the pearl.

Meanwhile, Golden Phoenix saw the bright light in the sky and shouted, "Look, Jade Dragon, isn't that the light from our pearl?"

Jade Dragon looked up from the Celestial River and said, "Yes it is!"

They followed the light to the palace of the Queen Mother of the West. There they found the pearl surrounded by admirers. "This is our pearl," Jade Dragon and Golden Phoenix shouted as they made their way through the crowd.

"How dare you say it's yours!" the enraged Queen Mother of the West shouted back. "I'm the mother of the Heavenly Emperor and all treasures belong to me."

The Queen Mother of the West clutched the tray tightly while ordering her palace guards to throw out Jade Dragon and Golden Phoenix. But they fought their way back, determined to retrieve the pearl. All three struggled over the golden tray, until the pearl fell off, dropping to the earth. When it touched the ground, the pearl immediately turned into a clear lake. Unable to part from it, Jade Dragon and Golden Phoenix changed themselves into two mountains that, to this day, stand by the lake.

And if you travel to China today, you can visit the famous West Lake, where the Jade Dragon and the Golden Phoenix stand by their precious pearl.

illustration by Heather Snitzer

Tiger Finds a Teacher

ONCE UPON A TIME, there was a tiger who lived deep in the mountains. He was very strong, but, since he was very clumsy, he rarely caught any animals.

One day as he left his cave to look for food, he saw a cat running down the mountain side. Tiger envied Cat's swift, easy movements and thought to himself, "I wish I were as clever as that cat!" He went to Cat and pleaded, "Dear Teacher Cat, will you teach me how to climb the mountain as well as you do?"

Knowing that tigers are wicked, Cat was afraid that if she taught him all she knew, her own life would be in danger. So she shook her head and said, "You'll use your knowledge to catch me."

Tiger bowed deeply to the cat. "Dear Cat," he said, "I honor my promises. If you will be so kind as to teach me, I promise that you can trust me. And afterward, if anyone should bully you, I'll take care of him for you."

Hearing these words, Cat was sympathetic. She tilted her head to one side and said, "All right. If you really promise that you will not be ungrateful, I'll teach you."

Tiger was overjoyed. He waved his tail and knelt down in front of her, saying, "In the future, when I have mastered all of the tricks of climbing hills and catching animals, I shall never forget you. May lightning strike me if I am ever unkind to you!"

He kept his word for some time, and treated Cat as one should treat a teacher. Every day from dawn to dusk Cat did her best to teach her pupil. Very soon she had taught him all her tricks except one. Tiger was very pleased with himself, and highly satisfied with Cat as a teacher.

Then one day, when he came to his teacher for further instruction, he looked at the Cat's plump body and his mouth began to water. What a good meal she would make! But Cat was fully aware of his bad intentions. She decided to give him a test.

"I have taught you all I know," she said. "Lessons are over."

Tiger thought his chance had come. "Aha!" he said to himself. "This fat little cat cannot escape my claws now!" But he thought he had better make sure that he had not misunderstood her, so he asked again, "Dear Teacher Cat, are you sure you have taught me everything?"

"Yes, everything!" said the wily cat.

An idea flashed into Tiger's head and his eyes sparkled. "Teacher," said he, "What is that there on the tree?" As Cat turned her head to look, Tiger, his jaws open and his claws out, pounced on her. But just as quickly Cat ran up the tree.

Cat sat up in the tree, and said indignantly, "Well! You ungrateful creature! It was lucky for me that I was sensible enough not to teach you how to climb trees. If I had taught you that, you would have eaten me by now."

Tiger flew into a rage and tried to jump up into the tree, but he did not know how to climb it. He tried to bite the wood, but the trunk was too thick. Cat skipped about in the branches, teasing him by sitting down to wash or looking at him. Tiger grew angrier and angrier, but there was nothing he could do. Finally Cat jumped to another tree, and then another, until she had vanished.

All Tiger's wicked schemes came to naught, and all he could do was to make his way up the mountain again.

illustration by Yumiko Konishi

Who Has Lost His Tail?

THERE ONCE WAS A BIG banyan tree beside a brook, and on it a little monkey swung from branch to branch. A pair of butterflies fluttered by, and Little Monkey slid down the tree and chased after them. He jumped up to catch one, but just missed. He tripped over a pile of stones and fell down.

As he got to his feet, Little Monkey saw something long and slender lying on a rock. He looked closer and saw that it was a tail. It suddenly occurred to him that it could be his own tail, which may had fallen off when he fell. He quickly felt his rear, but his tail was still there. He wagged it just to make sure. He worried about the owner of the tail, and decided to go and look for him.

Little Monkey saw a dragonfly and said, "Hey! Dragonfly, stop! I picked up this tail a little while ago. Is it yours?"

Dragonfly laughed heartily. "We dragonflies don't have tails."

"But what's that long thing at the end of your body. Isn't it a tail?"

Dragonfly said, "No. It's my belly. You'd better ask Carp whose tail that is."

Little Monkey called from the bank of the brook, "Carp! Is this your tail?"

Hearing Little Monkey call, Carp surfaced and answered, "No, it isn't mine. If ever I lost my tail, I would be like a boat without its rudder. I wouldn't be able to swim without a tail!" She then flipped her tail and dove into the clear water.

Little Monkey continued walking. Looking up, he saw Squirrel on a branch.

Little Monkey called to him, "Squirrel, I've picked up a tail. Is it yours?"

Squirrel leapt down and landed on the ground next to Little Monkey. "No, it isn't mine. Without my tail, I would not be able to jump from trees. My tail works like a parachute. My tail also keeps me warm at night."

Little Monkey said good-bye to Squirrel and continued his search. He looked everywhere for the tail's owner, but all animals he asked denied that it was theirs. There was nothing for him to do but return to the spot where he found the tail. He hung the tail in a tree and sat down, waiting for the owner to come back.

Little Monkey sat on a branch of a tree, still worrying about the tail, when suddenly he heard a magpie chatter, "Lizard's lost his tail!"

Little Monkey looked down, and saw the magpie making fun of a tail-less lizard. Happily, he seized the tail, leapt down, and with both hands offered the tail to Lizard. "Lizard, here you are. How did you manage without your tail?"

Lizard answered, "Quite well, actually. I didn't miss it at all."

Little Monkey scolded Lizard, "You don't realize how important a tail is. Without a tail, a carp cannot swim and a squirrel cannot jump down from a tree. And if I lost my tail, I could not swing on a tree very well. How could you possibly do without your tail?"

Lizard smiled and said, "Who said my tail isn't important? It saved my life. One afternoon a black snake snuck up behind me and caught my tail in his mouth. I shed my tail and got away, safe and sound. Don't worry. I can grow a new tail in no time."

Though Lizard did not take back his tail, Little Monkey felt as if he had rid himself of a heavy burden. He climbed up a tree and began swinging merrily to and fro.

illustration by Wendy K. Lee

Plop!

MANY, MANY YEARS AGO there were six rabbits who lived by a lake in the forest. One day, a big ripe fruit on a huge tree fell down into the lake, making a loud "plop!" when it hit the water. Not knowing what the noise could be, the rabbits were terrified and immediately raced off as fast as their four legs could carry them.

Fox saw them fleeing and asked, "Why are you running?"

Rabbit said, "Plop is coming!" When Fox heard this, he started to run with them. Next they ran into Monkey, who questioned, "Why are you in such a hurry?"

"Plop is coming!" replied Fox. So Monkey also joined their flight.

The news spread until Deer, Pig, Buffalo, Rhinoceros, Elephant, Black Bear, Brown Bear, Leopard, Tiger and Lion were all running away, helter-skelter. The faster they ran, the more frightened they became.

At the foot of a hill there lived another Lion with a long mane. When he saw the other lion running, he roared, "Brother Lion, you are the strongest of all animals. Why are you running like mad?"

"Plop is coming!" the running Lion panted.

"Who's Plop? Where is he?" Lion with the long mane demanded.

"Well, I don't really know." the other

stammered.

"Let's find out who it is then. Who told you about Plop?" said Lion.

"Tiger told me." answered the other lion.

Long-maned Lion asked Tiger, who said that Leopard had told him. Lion turned to Leopard, and Leopard answered that he had heard it from Brown Bear. In this way, Brown Bear, Black Bear, Elephant, Rhinoceros, Buffalo, Pig, Deer and Monkey were all asked, and each of them said he was told by someone else. Finally Fox was questioned and he said, "The rabbits told me." Then Lion went up to the rabbits, who squeaked together:

"All of us heard Plop with our own ears. We'll show you where we heard him."

They led Lion to the lake and told him, "The terrible Plop is there."

Just at that moment another big fruit fell from the tree and dropped into the water with a resounding "plop!"

Lion laughed. "Look, everyone!" he said. "You've all seen what 'plop' is. It's only the sound of a fruit dropping into the water. What's so terrifying about that?"

They breathed a sigh of relief. The panic had been all for nothing and the animals of the forest learned that they should not believe everything they hear.

illustration by Quan Van Nguyen

Li Chi Slays the Serpent

THERE ARE MOUNTAINS in China that were once inhabited by a giant serpent. It kept the local people in a state of constant terror and had already killed many officials of nearby towns. Offerings of oxen and sheep did not satisfy the monster. By entering men's dreams and making its wishes known, it demanded young girls of twelve or thirteen to feast on.

Fearful and helpless, officials selected daughters of slaves or criminals and kept them until the appointed dates. One day in the eighth month of every year, they would deliver a girl to the mouth of the monster's cave, and the serpent would come out and swallow the victim. This continued for nine years, until nine girls had been devoured.

In the tenth year the officials had again begun to look for a girl to hold in readiness for the appointed time. One man, Li Tan, had raised six daughters and no sons. Li Chi, his youngest girl, responded to the search for a victim by volunteering.

Her parents refused to allow it, but she said, "Dear parents, you have no one to depend on, for having brought forth six daughters and not a single son, it is as if you were childless. (In ancient China, daughters were valued much less than sons) I cannot take care of you in your old age; I only waste your food and clothes. Since I'm no use to you alive, why shouldn't I give up my life a little sooner? What could be wrong in selling me to gain a bit of money for your-

selves?" But the father and mother loved her too much to consent, so she went in secret.

Li Chi then asked the authorities for a sharp sword and a snake-hunting dog. When the appointed day of the eighth month arrived, she journeyed to the cave, clutching the sword and leading the dog. Then she took several baskets of rice balls moistened with malt sugar and placed them at the mouth of the serpent's cave.

The serpent appeared. Its head was as large as a rice barrel; its eyes were like mirrors two feet across. Smelling the fragrance of the rice balls, it opened its mouth to eat them. Then Li Chi unleashed the snake-hunting dog, which bit hard into the serpent. Li Chi herself came up from behind and slashed the serpent with several deep cuts. The wounds hurt so terribly that the monster leaped into the open and died.

Li Chi went into the serpent's cave and recovered the skulls of the nine victims. She sighed as she brought them out, saying, "Because you were afraid to fight, you quietly lost your lives. How sad!" Slowly she made her way homeward.

The king of the state of Yueh learned of these events and made Li Chi his queen. He made her father a high official, and her family was given riches. From that time forth, the area was free of monsters. Ballads celebrating Li Chi survive to this day.

illustration by Daniele Fraboulet

Other Books of Related Interest

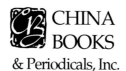